ENGLISH
AND PROUD OF IT

WILLIAM MOORE

summersdale

ENGLISH AND PROUD OF IT

Copyright © Summersdale Publishers Ltd, 2014

With research by Malcolm Croft

Summersdale Publishers Ltd
46 West Street
Chichester
West Sussex
PO19 1RP
UK

www.summersdale.com

Printed and bound in the Czech Republic

ISBN: 978-1-84953-521-2

Substantial discounts on bulk quantities of Summersdale books are available to corporations, professional associations and other organisations. For details contact Nicky Douglas by telephone: +44 (0) 1243 756902, fax: +44 (0) 1243 786300 or email: nicky@summersdale.com.

CONTENTS

INTRODUCTION

From the rolling, deep-green countryside of the Cotswolds to the country's cathedrals and castles, and from the world-famous Globe Theatre to the stunning landscapes of the Lake District and the meandering beauty of the River Thames – and everything in between – this little book will take you on a tour of everything that makes England terrific.

This beautiful country is the perfect getaway location – even if you live there! So, what are you waiting for, come and join us on a fantastic journey through the land of Michael Caine, William Shakespeare and Guy Fawkes, and discover what makes people English… and proud of it!

MAKING
HISTORY

IMPORTANT DATES
IN OUR HISTORY

Every **23 April**, England unites to celebrate its patron saint, George. His emblem, a red cross on a white background, is the unofficial flag of England and makes up part of the Union Jack – the official flag of the United Kingdom. During the crusades, St George's emblem was stitched into the knights' tunics so they could identify their fellow king's men in battle.

Before Hastings, the single most important
battle in England was the bloody Battle
of Brunanburh, near Burnley. It was
the conflict that determined whether
Britain would become one country or
remain as four separate ones. The year
was AD **937** and the Scots, Welsh and
Norse-Irish had all ganged up on the
Anglo-Saxons of King Æthelstan. The
Anglo-Saxons won – an important victory
in terms of establishing England and
Englishness as they are known today.

The stately homes
of England!
How beautiful they stand,
Amidst their tall
ancestral trees,
O'er all the pleasant land!

FELICIA DOROTHEA HEMANS

One of the most famous, and important, dates in English history: **14 October 1066**. When King Edward 'the Confessor' died earlier that year, he left no heirs and his death ignited a fierce rivalry for the throne that culminated in the historic Battle of Hastings and the ultimate destruction of the Anglo-Saxon rule of England. The Norman king, William, conquered the English and changed the country forever.

Liverpool was once one of England's most crucial cities. Its official history began on **28 August 1207**, when King John granted a Royal Charter for a place called 'Liuerpul' – even though only around two hundred people lived there at the time. Liverpool was once described as the 'Second City of Empire', eclipsing even London for commerce. Now Liverpool holds the Guinness World Records title for being the 'Capital of Pop', having secured more number one hits, than any other city in the UK. It is also one of the most passionate footballing cities in England; home to both Liverpool and Everton.

To put it mildly, the Magna Carta was a powerful document. When forced to sign it in **1215**, King John effectively limited his own powers and gave way to the formation of parliament as we now know it. The document was a collection of laws that would turn out to be the first vital step in creating constitutional government and law in the English-speaking world.

I know an
Englishman,
Being flattered,
is a lamb;
threatened, a lion.

GEORGE CHAPMAN

The English Civil War of **1642–1651** was one of the bitterest battles in the country's history – and there was certainly nothing civil about it. It was a fight between Royalists (aka Cavaliers, those who supported King Charles I) and Parliamentarians (aka Roundheads, led by Oliver Cromwell). The latter won, resulting in the temporary abolition of the English monarchy, the execution of King Charles I and, most tragically, the cancellation of Christmas in 1647 (it turned out Oliver Cromwell was a bit of a spoilsport).

Published on **15 April 1755**, Samuel Johnson's *A Dictionary of the English Language* was a milestone for the language that was soon to become one of the most spoken languages on the planet. Containing over 40,000 words, it took Johnson eight years to complete. The *Oxford English Dictionary* now has over 600,000 words (but the OED team enjoy more sophisticated production techniques than Johnson did).

21 October 1805 marks the date of the Battle of Trafalgar, the most decisive British naval victory of the Napoleonic War. The battle lasted only five hours and cost the Franco–Spanish fleet twenty-two ships, with the British navy losing no ships at all – 22–0!

Let no one sneer at the bruisers of England – What were the gladiators of Rome or the bull fighters of Spain, in its palmist days, compared to England's bruisers?

GEORGE BORROW

Wembley Stadium. England v. West Germany. **30 July 1966**. The FIFA World Cup Final. Geoff Hurst's hat-trick. *That* goal. 4–2 to England. They think it's all over… it is now!

In **July 2012**, London became the first city to have hosted the Olympic Games three times. The Games featured 302 events, 204 different countries, and 10,500 athletes. For three glorious weeks, a tiny island was once again the toast of the world. Team GB finished in third place, behind the United States and China, with an impressive haul of sixty-five medals in total: twenty-nine gold, seventeen silver and nineteen bronze. Well done, everyone!

WE CAN BE HEROES

PEOPLE WE CAN BE PROUD TO CALL OUR OWN

To be an
Englishman is
to belong to the
most exclusive
club there is.

OGDEN NASH

Theoretical physicist **Stephen Hawking**'s universe-bending book, *A Brief History of Time* (1988), discusses the theories of life, the universe and everything in a way that a non-scientific reader can understand. It changed how the world saw its universe. Being diagnosed with motor neuron disease at the age of 21 did not stop this Oxford-born boy from becoming one of the world's most inspiring geniuses.

Queen Elizabeth II has been the head of the British monarchy as well as sixteen sovereign states for over half a century (and counting). She celebrated her Diamond Jubilee in 2012 with a massive party and the whole world gatecrashed. The Queen is one of the most well-travelled monarchs in history, having made over 300 official overseas visits to well over a hundred different countries.

Consistently voted the 'Greatest Briton Ever', **Winston Churchill** is also one of the most quoted men in history. As prime minister of Britain during World War Two (and again from 1951 to 1955), Churchill's wartime speeches became a symbol of everything Britain stood for and gave hope and courage to millions of people in Britain and around the world. A world icon, made in England.

England's rose and mother of princes William and Harry (and now grandmother of George), **Diana Spencer** married Prince Charles in 1981 and their fairy-tale wedding was watched live on TV by 750 million people. Her tragic death in a car crash in Paris in 1997 was mourned the world over.

O England! model to
thy inward greatness,
Like little body with a
mighty heart,
What might'st thou do, that
honour would thee do,
Were all thy children kind
and natural!
But see thy fault!

WILLIAM SHAKESPEARE

Often described as the father of artificial intelligence, **Alan Turing** was one of the first computer geniuses. During World War Two, he worked at Bletchley Park and was integral to the codebreaking of German ciphers; a process that probably helped shorten the war by two years. He had previously devised what came to be known as the 'Turing machine', a hypothetical device that could simulate the logic of algorithms and computation – in other words, the foundations of modern-day computing.

Isaac Newton is widely regarded as one of the most influential scientists to have ever lived. Born on Christmas Day in Lincolnshire in 1642, Newton was the first to formulate the laws of gravity and motion in his *Philosophiæ Naturalis Principia Mathematica*, published in 1687, considered by many to be the most important book in the history of science.

In England every man
ought to own a garden.
It's meant to be that way,
you feel it immediately.

HENRY MILLER

Florence Nightingale, recognised for her work in improving hospital hygiene and sanitation, was famously known as the 'Lady with the Lamp' because of her frequent visits to the hospital wards of the Crimea at night to check on patients. She laid the foundations of modern professional healthcare with her nursing school at St Thomas' Hospital, London, and in 1907 she became the first woman to be awarded the Order of Merit – an exclusive order recognising distinguished service in the armed forces, science, art, literature or the promotion of culture.

Born in 1809, the English naturalist **Charles Darwin** was one of the first biologists to popularise the theory of natural selection – the idea that every living creature on earth evolved from inherited characteristics of previous species and organisms. Darwin's influential book *On the Origin of Species*, published in 1859, is considered the foundation of evolutionary biology.

What have I done for you,
England, my England?
What is there I would not do,
England, my own?

W. E. HENLEY

Alfred, King of Wessex was also known as King of the Anglo-Saxons and as **Alfred the Great** – but no matter what you call him, he was undeniably the first true king of England – even before 'England' existed. He ruled the land from 871 to 899 and defended his people and his kingdom against those pesky Viking marauders. A learned and merciful man, who encouraged education and improved his kingdom's legal system and military structure, Alfred the Great was indeed just that.

The English have an
extraordinary ability for
flying into a great calm.

ALEXANDER WOOLLCOTT

SOMETHING TO REMEMBER US BY

OUR NATION'S CULTURAL HIGHLIGHTS

Launched in 1511, the beautiful **Mary Rose** was designed as the flagship of King Henry VIII's fleet. Sadly, for reasons still unknown, on 19 July 1545 she sank in the Solent whilst leading other ships out to face the French. The ship remained buried under water, a perfect Tudor-era time capsule, for over 400 years until, on 11 October 1982, the wreck was raised and salvaged. She now resides at Portsmouth Historic Dockyard.

The **London Underground** celebrated its 150th birthday in 2013, and over one billion passengers travelled across the much-loved transport network that year alone. Out of a total of 270 stations, the District Line (the green one) has the most (sixty). Despite being known colloquially around the world as 'the Tube', only 45 per cent of the Underground track network actually runs through tunnels.

An Englishman,
even if he is
alone, forms
an orderly
queue of one.

GEORGE MIKES

Although the Chinese nicknamed it Da Ben Zhong, which when translated means 'Big Stupid Clock', **Big Ben** is far more than that. Over 150 years old, the huge clock tower located at the Palace of Westminster took fifteen years to build. The name Big Ben refers not to this clock tower, printed on so many London postcards, but instead to the 13-ton bell housed within it. The name of the tower itself was changed from the Clock Tower to the Elizabeth Tower in honour of the Queen's Diamond Jubilee in 2012.

York Minster as we know it today is a feat of fifteenth-century engineering and is one of the largest cathedrals not just in England, but also in Europe. The Central Tower (also known as the Lantern Tower) is a staggering 70 metres (230 feet) tall and weighs the same as forty jumbo jets – roughly 16,000 metric tonnes. It has to be seen to be enjoyed.

Summer afternoon – summer afternoon; to me those have always been the two most beautiful words in the English language.

HENRY JAMES

Whenever you lie back and dream of the rolling, gently dipping green hillsides of England you may well be thinking of **the Cotswolds** in southern England. The Cotswolds cover an area 40 kilometres (25 miles) across and 145 kilometres (90 miles) long. The region has been designated an Area of Outstanding Natural Beauty due, in part, to the honey-coloured limestone that permeates the entire region, giving the village and town architecture a distinct and quintessentially English feel.

An area of extreme natural beauty, the **Lake District**, located in Cumbria in northern England, is the largest national park in the country. The lakes and the fells were carved out by huge glaciers that eroded the landscape before melting away. Around 14 million people a year visit the national park, but, thankfully, they don't all go there at once.

It was one of
those perfect
English autumnal
days which occur
more frequently
in memory
than in life.

P. D. JAMES

The **White Cliffs of Dover** form part of the English coastline facing out to the Strait of Dover and over to France. At their highest the cliffs reach 110 metres (350 feet), and they are an arresting and welcoming sight for any traveller from continental Europe.

The cliffs are white because they are made up of the crushed shells of billions of tiny sea creatures that, over millions of years, have risen up as chalk sediment.

The Queen's official London residence,
Buckingham Palace, is a building of
rare beauty. Originally built in 1705 as a
townhouse for the Duke of Buckingham
(hence the name), the palace has since
been extended to include 775 rooms,
1,514 doors, 760 windows and 40,000
light bulbs. It covers 77,000 square metres
and has its own postcode – SW1A 1AA.
And you can always tell when the queen
is home – the official flag, known as the
Royal Standard, flies at full mast on top
of the palace when she is in residence.

Good ale, the true and proper drink of Englishmen. He is not deserving of the name of Englishman who speaketh against ale, that is good ale.

GEORGE BORROW

Stonehenge, near Salisbury, is one of the most important prehistoric sites in the world. The construction and pattern of the peculiar standing stones began roughly around 2500 BC and the freestanding structures were probably used for religious, burial and ceremonial purposes. Evidence suggests the large stones were brought all the way from the Preseli Hills in Wales – around 200 miles away. In 1986, Stonehenge was added to UNESCO's coveted list of World Heritage Sites, which must have made the Queen very happy indeed – she owns the place!

In the heart of Westminster, a stone's throw from the Houses of Parliament, lies the nation's venue for coronations and royal weddings, and the resting place of seventeen monarchs, **Westminster Abbey**. Building was begun by King Henry III (though not personally) in 1245 and the soaring Gothic architecture became a splendid sight to behold. The abbey is also thought to be home to England's oldest door – made of oak, it dates back to AD 1050.

There is nothing so bad or so good that you will not find an Englishman doing it; but you will never find an Englishman in the wrong. He does everything on principle.

GEORGE BERNARD SHAW

STARS IN OUR EYES

THE ENTERTAINERS WE LOVE

Selling over one and a half billion records (and counting), **The Beatles** are consistently regarded to be the most successful and influential music group of all time. Formed in 1960 in Liverpool, John Lennon, Paul McCartney, George Harrison and Ringo Starr had seventeen Number One singles in only six years – their first, 'From Me To You', was written while on a coach travelling to Shrewsbury in 1963. Rock and roll!

Since bounding onto British TVs in 1999 with a little show called *The Naked Chef*, **Jamie Oliver** is now one of England's most popular exports. He has sold over ten million cookbooks worldwide and, most recently, has been on a daring mission to educate Britain about its naughty eating habits (see chapter 6). He was voted the 'Most Inspiring Political Figure of 2005' by a Channel 4 News viewer poll and in 2003 was awarded an MBE.

In truth, no men on earth
can cheer like Englishmen,
who do so rally one
another's blood and spirit
when they cheer in earnest,
that the stir is like the rush
of their whole history.

CHARLES DICKENS

No other actor epitomises Englishness like Londoner **Michael Caine**. Having starred in over 100 films, Caine has been nominated for an Oscar six times and has won twice. Can you name the two films? His famous cockney accent has graced such internationally successful films as *Zulu* (1964), *Alfie* (1966), *The Italian Job* (1969) and, more recently, *The Dark Knight* trilogy (2005–2012). All together now, 'My name is Michael Caine…'

His career now spanning seven decades, **Cliff Richard** is one of England's most popular entertainers. He has sold over 250 million albums, 21 million in the UK alone. A national treasure, Richard's real name is Harry Rodger Webb. In September 2013, Richard released his hundredth album!

I travelled among
unknown men,
In lands beyond the sea:
Nor England! Did I
know till then
What love I bore to thee.

WILLIAM WORDSWORTH

Robbie Williams, one of England's favourite entertainers in recent years, is also the UK's most successful male solo artist ever. Also a member of boy band Take That (twice), Williams has sold over 70 million records and sold out his 2006 'Close Encounters' tour of 1.6 million tickets in a single day – a Guinness World Record, still unbeaten. One of his biggest singles, 'Let Me Entertain You', has been played on radio over four million times.

By this sacredness of individuals, the English have in seven hundred years evolved the principles of freedom.

RALPH WALDO EMERSON

Billionaire **Richard Branson** is one of the world's most high-profile, successful and fascinating entrepreneurs. Since beginning to trade in the music record business in the early 1970s, he has since set up Virgin Atlantic, Virgin Records, Virgin Trains, Virgin Cola, Virgin Active and Virgin Galactic, to name but a few. The latter intends to be the first company to provide suborbital spaceflights to space tourists. Book your ticket now!

David Attenborough's stunning nature programmes have entertained and enthralled British TV audiences for the past sixty years. A national treasure and all-round lovely Englishman, Attenborough was included by viewers in the BBC's 2002 poll to find the '100 Greatest Britons'. He was knighted by the Queen in 1985.

An Englishman's
home is his castle.
ENGLISH PROVERB

Whether you love him or loathe him, there is no doubting his domination of British telly. Lambeth-born **Simon Cowell**, with his *The X Factor* and *Britain's Got Talent* reality shows (and their US equivalents), has flooded television for the past ten years, propelling internationally successful acts such as Leona Lewis, One Direction, Paul Potts and Susan Boyle to worldwide stardom.

Outlasting The Beatles by over forty years, **The Rolling Stones** are England's most enduring rock band. Now in their fifth decade, the Stones have conquered all areas of the globe with their rebellious rock 'n' roll. They have sold over 250 million albums to date and there is still much life left in them judging by their first-ever Glastonbury headline appearance in 2013.

If I could create an ideal world, it would be an England with the fire of the Elizabethans, the correct taste of the Georgians, and the refinement and pure ideals of the Victorians.

H. P. LOVECRAFT

English footballing hero **David Beckham** is without doubt one of the most loved players of any generation. His skills on the pitch are legendary, not least his ability to score with free kicks from any angle or distance. He also owns one of the most recognised faces on the planet and, whether as a global fashion icon or as a UNICEF Goodwill Ambassador, the English people are full of pride to have him on their side.

THE WRITE STUFF

STUFF

FAMOUS WRITERS, POETS AND PLAYWRIGHTS

William Shakespeare is, of course, the greatest English writer ever to have put quill to parchment. Famously dying on the same day he was born (fifty-two years apart), Shakespeare's output of comedies, tragedies, histories and sonnets defined the sixteenth and seventeenth centuries in which he lived. His *Macbeth* has been performed on stage more than any other play ever written. On average, there is a performance of the play somewhere in the world every four hours.

Geoffrey Chaucer lived between 1343 and 1400 and is often hailed as the Father of English Literature and the greatest poet of the Middle Ages. Chaucer's *The Canterbury Tales* was the first work to be written in Middle English (back then most writing was in French or Latin) and is therefore credited with popularising English as the vernacular language of the nation. *The Canterbury Tales* describes the story of a group of pilgrims as they travel from Southwark, London, to Canterbury Cathedral.

England expects
that every man
will do his duty.

HORATIO NELSON

Unarguably the best-selling novelist of all time, **Agatha Christie** has sold – according to *Guinness World Records* – over four billion books, spanning her sixty-six crime novels. This puts her stories behind only the works of Shakespeare and the Bible as the most widely published books ever. The Belgian detective Hercule Poirot (he of the magnificent moustache) and the elderly spinster Miss Marple are Christie's most famous character creations, and she also wrote *The Mousetrap*, the world's longest-running play. Not bad for a girl from Devon.

Charles John Huffam Dickens is one of England's most beloved authors. *Oliver Twist* and *Great Expectations*, to name but two of his works, are classics of the English Literature canon, revered for their use of powerful adjectives, rhythmic quality (great for reading out loud), metaphors and similes. He was truly a master of the written word. Dickens is also considered responsible for restoring merriment to Christmas celebrations, after *A Christmas Carol* (1843) reinstated the Christmas customs of ye olde merrie England to the nation's cultural consciousness.

England was full of words I'd never heard before – streaky bacon, short back and sides, serviettes, high tea, ice-cream cornet.

BILL BRYSON

One of three famous siblings,
Emily Brontë wrote her one and only
novel, *Wuthering Heights* (1847), under
the pseudonym Ellis Bell. This classic story
of love and jealousy between Catherine
and Heathcliff, set around a Yorkshire
moorland farmhouse, is one of English
literature's finest moments. Brontë died
the year after it was first published.

Charlotte Brontë's *Jane Eyre* tells the heart-a-fluttering tale of the burgeoning maturity of the titular hero, and her blossoming love for Mr Rochester has been the cause of much weeping and wonder all around the world. Published in 1847, the novel was published under Brontë's pen name, Currer Bell. Charlotte Brontë, of course was also the sister of Anne and Emily Brontë – truly a family that has contributed greatly to English literature.

So many of the loveliest things in England are melancholy.

DODIE SMITH

If you have never read any of **Jane Austen**'s books, don't worry – you've probably seen all the films. Born in Steventon, Hampshire in 1775, Austen was the author of the revered *Sense and Sensibility* (1811), *Pride and Prejudice* (1813), *Mansfield Park* (1814) and *Emma* (1816). These widely read tales of romantic fiction and her clever wit have gained her a place as one of the country's greatest ever writers, with a dedicated fanbase that extends all over the world.

Published in 1937, **J. R. R. Tolkien's** *The Hobbit* is the classic children's story of Bilbo Baggins' journey from the Shire across Middle-earth to take back golden treasures from the ancient and terrifying dragon, Smaug. Its sequel, *The Lord of the Rings*, has sold over 150 million copies and been translated into over fifty languages. Both works have been made into successful film series by director Peter Jackson. Not satisfied with his achievements as a writer, poet and university professor, Tolkien spent any free afternoons he had on one of his other passions – philology, the invention and development of language.

The south-west wind roaring
in from the Atlantic…
is, I think, the presiding
genius of England.

HILAIRE BELLOC

Published under the gender-ambiguous pen name of **J. K. Rowling**, Joanne Rowling's first book *Harry Potter and the Philosopher's Stone* was a publishing game-changer. Its success spawned a series of seven books chronicling the battles and journey into adulthood of the young wizard Harry and his friends at Hogwarts, all the while fighting off the evil wizard, He-who-shall-not-be-named (Voldemort). The *Harry Potter* series of books has sold over 450 million copies… so far.

Mary Shelley started writing her magnum opus, *Frankenstein,* at just eighteen years of age, but it went on to influence literature, film and popular culture for the next century. It also gave the world one of the most inspired, and frightening, monster creations ever known, famed for such chilling lines as, 'If I cannot inspire love, I will cause fear!'

Her mother called her **Isabella Mary Beeton**, but we all know and love her as simply Mrs Beeton. Celebrated as not only one of the first and best cookery writers that England has ever produced, Mrs Beeton was also the author of the famous guidebook on how to maintain a house in Victorian Britain – *Mrs Beeton's Book of Household Management* – a tome that single-handedly created a genre of publishing that fills bookshop shelves to this day.

FOOD FOR THOUGHT

OUR LANDMARK DISHES

The mighty Sunday **roast beef** (with roast potatoes, Yorkshire pudding, gravy and fifteen types of vegetables, naturally) has been feeding the English for over 500 years, so much so that the French call us *rosbifs* and the royal bodyguards, the Yeoman Warders who protect the Tower of London, are called 'Beefeaters'. A portion of roast beef with all the trimmings contains, on average, 800 calories – not including seconds!

Cumberland sausages with fluffy mashed potato (or lumpy mashed potato if you prefer), served with lashings of rich onion gravy. There is nothing more English than **bangers and mash**. Bangers confirmed their explosive nickname during World War Two when, due to rationing, sausages had a high water content and were therefore liable to blow up when cooking.

Be England what she will. With all her faults, she is my country still.

CHARLES CHURCHILL

Two slices of thick white toast, two slices of bacon, two sausages, black pudding (if you dare!), mushrooms, tomatoes, two fried eggs and ladles of steaming baked beans. Wars have been won on the **full English breakfast**, which sometimes goes by the name of the 'full monty'.

The legendary double act of fried
fish and chips was first served on
English shores, quite literally, sometime
around the middle of the nineteenth
century. There are currently around ten
thousand 'chippies' taking orders in
Britain, with cod being the most popular
dish of the day – it accounts for 61 per
cent of all over-the-counter sales.

The English
contribution to
world cuisine
– the chip.

JOHN CLEESE

Kippers have been putting hair on the chest of any Englishman who dares to eat them for decades. Prepared with whole herrings, these small oily fish are butterflied from head to tail along the dorsal and then gutted, salted and smoked. You can dollop a poached egg on top, if you fancy. A very fishy dish… but incredibly nutritious.

Essentially a Sunday roast covered in a thick doorstop pastry, **Cornish pasties** have been enjoyed in England for donkey's years. In the eighteenth century pasties were the dish of the day for Cornish miners, because it allowed them to take their lunch down the mine – the pastry protected the meat, potato, swede, onion and gravy filling and was thrown away after they had sucked the insides dry.

Good apple
pies are a
considerable part
of our domestic
happiness.

JANE AUSTEN

Bacon butty – the best hangover food in the world thanks to the high salt content of the four slices of bacon every great butty should possess. The amino acids produced by bacon also top up your neurotransmitters, which are vital to clearing your head. A bacon butty was recently voted the nation's favourite food. Do you agree?

Toad-in-the-hole should perhaps be kept in a museum, such is its status as one of the most traditional dishes of English cuisine. Juicy hot sausages surrounded by Yorkshire pudding batter, served with gravy and veg – it is a masterpiece of simplicity. WARNING! The French version of this dish is *completely* different (the crazy fools attempt to achieve the same effect by cracking eggs inside the holes that they gouge from slices of bread).

And laughter,
learnt of friends;
and gentleness,
In hearts at
peace, under an
English heaven.

RUPERT BROOKE

Cured pork meat + pork jelly + crusty pastry = **pork pies**. This Russian doll of a pre-dinner treat is one of England's favourite snacks. Indeed, the pork pie industry in England alone is worth more than £145 million annually. Who eats all the pies? WE DO!

To this great
cause of Freedom
drink, my friends,
And the great
name of England
round and round.

ALFRED, LORD TENNYSON

Bubble and squeak is a tasty mishmash of Sunday roast leftovers (but usually just the veg), which are shallow-fried until golden brown. The name derives from the sound the leftovers make when combined and cooked in the pan – an enticing bubbling and squeaking that makes the mouth salivate like one of Pavlov's dogs.

MAPPING THE NATION

OUR WEATHER AND GEOGRAPHY

The atlas, as we know it, is not always as correctly proportioned as it might be. **England** is actually seventy-four times smaller than the USA, fifty-nine times smaller than Australia and three times smaller than Japan.

The **highest temperature ever recorded**
in England was 38.5 ºC (101.3 ºF) in
Brogdale, Kent, on 10 August 2003.
Hopefully you were near a beach that day.

When two
Englishmen meet
their first talk is
of the weather.

SAMUEL JOHNSON

The **largest natural lake** in England is the mesmerising Windermere in the Lake District, Cumbria. It measures just over 18 kilometres (11 miles) in length and has a depth of 67 metres (219 feet), but no Nessie-esque monsters have been sighted. Yet.

England's highest point is Scafell Pike at 978 metres (3,209 feet), and it can be found in the Lake District National Park, in Cumbria. It is six times smaller than Mount Everest, but please don't hold that against it.

I hope for nothing in this world so ardently as once again to see that paradise called England.

COSIMO III, GRAND DUKE OF TUSCANY

Holme Fen in Cambridgeshire is the
lowest-lying point in England, registering
2.75 metres (9 feet) below sea level.
Amazingly, over 500 species of fungi
can be found in this ancient bog.

The **longest river** in England is the serpent-shaped River Thames, traditionally considered to run from a remote Gloucestershire meadow on the edge of a small village called Kemble, and flowing easterly to the North Sea. It is 346 kilometres (215 miles) long and home to over 100 species of fish and over five species of supermarket trolley.

This blessed plot,
this earth,
this realm,
this England.

WILLIAM SHAKESPEARE

The **longest period of constant rainfall** in England happened between 13 and 15 June 1903 in Central London – it fell for fifty-nine hours straight. It is estimated that 161 millimetres (6.3 inches) of rain fell, or put another way, approximately 288 million tons (64 billion gallons) of water.

There is nothing about which I am more anxious than my country, and for its sake I am willing to die ten deaths, if that be possible.

ELIZABETH I

The **lowest monthly total of sunshine**
ever recorded in England was – wait
for it – 0 hours in Westminster, London,
in December 1890. Unbelievable
or unsurprising – you decide!

The **highest monthly sunshine total**
ever recorded in England was 383.9
hours in Eastbourne, Sussex, in July 1911.
Suncream was invented in 1944, a tad
too late for this particular heatwave.

THE OBJECTS OF OUR DESIRE

ICONIC OBJECTS AND FAMOUS INVENTIONS

Tim Berners-Lee, a computer scientist and engineer born in south-west London in 1955, is credited with the invention of the **World Wide Web** in 1989. Berners-Lee gave the www to the world for free, with no patents and made available on royalty-free technology, so that it could be used and adopted by anyone.

The flag of England since the Middle Ages is the **St George's Cross** – a red cross on a white background. While the flag has no official status within the United Kingdom (it was adopted into the Union Jack in 1606), the St George's flag flies regularly and proudly at many sporting events to this day and is the most iconic symbol of English national pride.

The genius Isaac Newton did more than just formulate the laws of gravity and motion – he also invented and built the first working **reflecting telescope** in 1668. Reflecting telescopes use curved mirrors, whereas the old-school refracting telescopes had used a lens. All the modern-day telescopes used in astronomy are based on Newton's initial reflecting telescope, as will be the world's largest ever telescope, the European Extremely Large Telescope (E-ELT), which is currently being built in Chile. Newton would be proud.

But, after all, what would
the English be without their
sweet unreasonableness.

JOHN GALSWORTHY

Introduced in 1947, a London **black cab** is one of England's internationally renowned icons, as quintessentially English as fish and chips and bowler hats. Interestingly, all black cabs were in fact initially designed to be tall enough to accommodate anybody wearing a bowler hat! All taxicab drivers in London must pass 'The Knowledge' – a rigorous test that involves memorising 320 routes, 25,000 streets and 20,000 landmarks within a 6-mile radius around Charing Cross.

English people used to get a lot of stick about the state of their teeth. This seems a trifle unfair considering it was an Englishman called William Addis who, in 1780 at a factory in Whitechapel, East London, invented and mass-produced the first **toothbrush** as we now know it.

The English
never draw a
line without
blurring it.

WINSTON CHURCHILL

Perhaps the reason English people used to get a reputation for having bad teeth is because they also invented the **chocolate bar**. In 1847, the Fry's chocolate factory in Bristol became the first company to mould and mass-produce a chocolate bar, and they also produced the first chocolate Easter egg in the UK in 1873. Smile!

Born in Gloucester in 1871, Hubert Cecil Booth (a very English name if ever there was one) invented the first 'motorised' **vacuum cleaner** in 1901. While another English inventor, James Dyson, may owe him a multi-billion pound debt of gratitude, thankfully we don't!

Mad dogs and
Englishmen
go out in the
midday sun.
NOËL COWARD

In 1934 English inventor Percy Shaw came up with the rather splendid idea of '**cat's eyes**', the anything-but-middle-of-the-road idea for lighting up the middle of the road while driving at night. A simple invention, yes, but it revolutionised the transport industry.

In 1680 an Englishman called William Dockwra established the London Penny Post, a pre-Royal Mail company that delivered letters and parcels inside the City of London for the measly sum of one penny. Though the letter or parcel itself was not stamped, a separate piece of paper accompanying the letter was. This piece of paper is considered by many historians to be the world's first **postage stamp**.

The people of
England are the
most enthusiastic
in the world.

BENJAMIN DISRAELI

As a nation of fanatical tea-drinkers – around 60 billion cups of tea are sipped each year in Britain – it was perhaps inevitable that one of them would invent the **automatic electric kettle** and, in October 1955, Englishman Peter Hobbs (the Hobbs of the ubiquitous Russell Hobbs design company) did just that. His original design, the K1, now resides in the London Science Museum. Next time you have a brew, raise your cup or mug in salute.

An Englishman
never enjoys
himself, except
for a noble
purpose.
ALAN PATRICK HERBERT

A LAW UNTO OURSELVES

THE PECULIAR LAWS THAT KEEP US OUT OF TROUBLE

Despite the government slashing 45,000 laws from the statutes in 2006, it is still, under the Salmon Act 1986, illegal to 'handle salmon in suspicious circumstances'.

I like the English.
They have the
most rigid code
of immorality
in the world.

MALCOLM BRADBURY

The 1313 Statute Forbidding Bearing of
Armour forbids any Member of Parliament
to wear armour in the House of Lords.

Under section 60 of the Metropolitan
Police Act 1839 it is illegal to beat or shake
any carpet or rug in any street in England.
(However, beating or shaking a
doormat is allowed before 8 a.m.)

Not only England,
but every
Englishman
is an island.

NOVALIS

Under the Tax Avoidance Schemes
Regulations 2006, it is illegal not to tell
the taxman anything you do not want
him to know, but legal not to tell him
information you do not mind him knowing.
(Confused?)

Under the Transport for London Railway Byelaws, it is illegal to 'jump' a queue located in a Tube-station hall. 'Any person directed to queue by an authorised person or a sign must join the rear of the queue and obey the reasonable instructions of any authorised person regulating the queue.'

Thank God for tea! What would the world do without tea? How did it exist? I am glad I was not born before tea.

REVEREND SYDNEY SMITH

According to the Protection of Wrecks (RMS *Titanic*) Order 2003, a person shall not enter the hull of the *Titanic* without permission from the Secretary of State.

Under the Wildlife and Countryside Act 1981, it is illegal to eat mute swan unless you're the Queen of the United Kingdom.

You often hear that the English climate has had a profound effect upon the English temperament. I don't believe it. I believe they were always like that.

WILL CUPPY

In Lancashire, no person is permitted,
after being asked to stop doing
so by a constable on the seashore,
to incite a dog to bark.

All Royal Navy ships that enter
the Port of London must officially
provide a barrel of rum to the
Constable of the Tower of London.

We don't take ourselves as seriously as some other countries do.

JOAN COLLINS

Under section 54 of the Metropolitan Police Act 1839 it is illegal to carry a plank of wood along a pavement. Other offences covered by section 54 include 'flying kites' and 'sliding on ice or snow in the street'.

THERE'S NO PLACE LIKE HOME

FAMOUS PLACES TO SEE AND THINGS TO DO

For over forty years Michael Eavis's
Glastonbury Festival at Worthy Farm in
Pilton, Somerset, has played host to the
biggest names in music from all around
the world. The cost of admittance to the
first ever festival was £1 and you got free
milk from the farm! One thousand five
hundred people turned up. Nowadays,
ticket prices are over £200 for a three-day
pass and around 170,000 people attend.

The **Eden Project** in St Austell, Cornwall, consists of multiple artificial biomes created in the crater of a disused china clay pit (the size of thirty-five football pitches!). Their purpose is to create a 'spectacular theatre in which to tell the story of human dependence on plants', and they are now home to millions of flora species collected from all around the planet.

The proper means of increasing the love we bear our native country is to reside some time in a foreign one.

WILLIAM SHENSTONE

The street artist Banksy has achieved international stardom over the past two decades for his anonymous and humorous – and sometimes downright genius – collection of social critiques in the form of graffiti. His hometown of Bristol now offers a **Banksy Walking Tour** that proudly shows off many of the early works that remain idolised by his counterculture followers.

Coopers Hill in Gloucestershire is home to the annual, and much-loved, **cheese-rolling competition**. The aim is simple: organisers roll a 9-lb wheel of Double Gloucester down a steep hill, and the winner is the first to catch it before the bottom of the hill or, if the cheese cannot be caught, to reach the finishing line first. The event dates back to the fifteenth century and long may it continue!

England is
unrivalled for two
things – sport
and politics.

BENJAMIN DISRAELI

As quintessentially English as they sound, the **World Gravy Wrestling Championships** are an event that started back in 2008. Every August Bank Holiday, near Bacup in Lancashire (home of England's best gravy and hotpot), fancy-dressed participants compete to become the World's Best Gravy Wrestler. It's yet to go professional, but around 1,500 people support the event, which was won in 2013 by a man dressed as a Yorkshire pudding.

The '**Ye Olde Trip to Jerusalem**', near the grounds of historic Nottingham Castle, lays serious claim to being England's oldest surviving inn, having served ale to all who have frequented its pokey corridors for over 800 years. Established around 1189, the inn gets its name from the medieval crusaders who rested there for refreshments before marching on to the Middle East.

The Needles lighthouse that sits rather perilously at the most westerly point of the Isle of Wight is truly a sight to behold – a tiny stick of red and white in a stormy sea of blue and grey set against a massive block of the white chalk that makes up the distinctive chemistry of the coastline there. Rising out of the sea like stalagmites, The Needles Rocks are a row of three chalk stacks that are one of the natural wonders of this craggy isle.

William Shakespeare's home from home, the original **Globe Theatre**, was built in 1599 in Southwark, London, but was all but destroyed by fire in 1613. In 1997, just down the road from the original site, an open-air reconstruction of the original opened its curtains to rapturous applause. If all the world's a stage, the Globe Theatre is the very centre of that world.

If you want
to eat well in
England, eat
three breakfasts.

W. SOMERSET MAUGHAM

Kensington's **Natural History Museum** opened on 18 April 1881. It is one of the largest and most prestigious museums in the world and boasts a collection of 55 million animal species, 28 million insects, 9 million fossils, 6 million plant species, 500 rocks and minerals and 3,200 meteorites. There are also some great gift shops.

Unlike golf, the path that passes by the **White Horse at Uffington** is not a good walk spoiled. In fact, the beautiful walk – taking in ancient England's rolling green hills – is along one of the country's oldest 'roads', the Ridgeway. According to legend, the White Horse is also near the hill-site where St George famously slayed that dragon. The views of the ancient hill fort of Uffington Castle aren't bad either.

Heaven take thy soul, and England keep my bones!

WILLIAM SHAKESPEARE

If you're interested in finding out more about our books, find us on Facebook at **Summersdale Publishers** and follow us on Twitter at **@Summersdale**.

www.summersdale.com